IN THE FORM OF IT

Mike Randall

BookLeaf Publishing

India | USA | UK

Presentation by *BookLeaf Publishing*

Web: www.bookleafpub.com

E-mail: info@bookleafpub.com

ISBN: 9789360944353

First edition 2024

Evening Song

Let us sing! Let us sing!
Despite
said the Shrike
of the Dark
and the Lark
agreed,
Let us sing

The one with the wooden antlers

It came in the bright light of daytime sky
In the form of a shrike like a pay-line fine
That measures each minute
The moment you spin it
Forever counting backwards from nine

It came in the dark
In the form of a lark
Its voice singing hymn songs unheard
Its wings beating rhythms that soared
Over the hillsides, the buildings, and cities'
Nocturnal cycle of pities

Its stems of its roses of infinite depth
Extending in motions of intimate breath
Like once supple branches of a now gnarled tree
Exposing, it shows it
The many long years yet to be

Sprouting from its temples, reaching up to the
stars
With trunks ever slender and most elegant bark
It flowers, and leaves
What will always foil in time

Though its roots be rooted deepest
In the most supple of soils:
The mind

The one with the sky for a mind

Its thoughts passed like clouds
And when it rained
Its memories
Saturated the soil
From which the trees grew out
To become the embodiment
Of everything it ever thought or felt

The one with the hourglass heart

It came to see how deep imagination grows
It came to make a world up, a world we came to
know

A vessel
Neither only evil
Nor of love
Did it hold in the bottom of its hourglass heart
But rather both
With balanced strength, in equal part

Its unmaking laid waiting in the sands
When its time had come,
Its beginning, middle, end
Danced forever, hand in hand

The sides of the container
Broke and fell away
And the empty space inside
Which had only arbitrary shape
Was now free to merge and blend
With all the rest of empty space

Equal and Opposing

Two godly forces
Equal in strength
Opposite in purpose

When tested against each other
The one that fights will lose
The one that loves the other's fight
Will be hit, but will not bruise

Ready on cue

Running on fumes in a vehicle
Not built for this terrain
Playing the role of side character
In the costume of the main

Painting pictures with words
In languages you don't understand
It's just an improv show;
but you wrote all the lines on your hand

The jester laughs at the joke you made
And the puppet moves your arm that way
Your mask is bent and torn -- but that's okay
Because it's not the face your face makes
anyway

Bird cry

Last of its kind,
it cries
First of its kind
to hear silence in reply

When we would cry
with tears, with eyes,
The songbird cries with its Cry
Its lows, its highs
Its melody unlike another

No such Cry
Is more a cry
Than that horrified
cry that mortifies;
The last cries of a species that dies

Last of its kind
it Cries
First of its kind
to hear silence in reply

They said to us:

"I made a rope ladder
from the silk pillowcase
I found my body wrapped in

As I climbed, I realized
it was not strong enough to bear the weight of
death;
My thoughts were too heavy.
So I let them drop

Desperately hoping
when they fell, and when they landed,
that they would stay broken,
unable to explode.
Unlike the unlikely thoughts
that fell on our home"

The Softness Above

The pastel palette
of an early winter day
before the first snow
but after the frost
that covers all in a subtle shine
Amplified
by the light dust of gold from the east.
And the subdued hues
from the low hanging fog
And the gradient bleeding outwards
from horizon
to the softness above

No Thing

Which holds more merit:
The sides of the container,
Or the Emptiness within it?

If needed to decide,
Would you take a house's walls,
Or the Space to live inside?

If Nothingness as the essence
Cannot exist alone,
Is it truly what it claims to be,
Or just part of the whole?

Meet us on the Ant Hill

The first church built
was made of silt
5,000 stories high
Red ants were its inhabitants
Harvesters of the sky

Before their gourmet flowers bloomed
They groomed their dormant powers, and soon
They began to dream
And they began to scheme
Then they began to weave
Together a set and screen

But then in an instant
Existence was tinted
a subtle hue
Someone bumped into it
Now it's tilted askew
by two in the Y and three in the Z
And the soundtrack abruptly changed key

hail to the LED flicker

Default mode melody can remain
as the alternating LED candle flame
Its on and off flicker at speeds it seems
unchanged
A light that's alight
only half of the time
In pictures that we keep estranged

We, the post-immortals,
once in steady flame
now stagger forwards
and dream
in cinema scenes
that flicker on from off
with nothing in between

The immortal ones
lived twice as long
with absent tongues and candles made of fire
they wept, for even gods must dream
but never slept
remembering what came prior

Brief Eternity

With each new day my history made in past
By sights my eyes entice and breathes I breathe
Carved in Time tested stone with words to last
The story, by my lives, behind me leave

Laws of wild land equate with all but me
When my paths cross with that of greater deeds
Like grains whose hands dare not embrace the
sea
Insufferable peons, we to hearts of galaxies

A fly's voice can scarcely pierce the void
Its wingbeat barely fill a gap in Time
Yet by our equally shorted lives,
Our moments, voices, become eternalized

With what there is

In a world of dust and charred remains
It comes as smoke, it comes as flame

In a world of handshakes and professional greed
It came in the profits that nobody needs

In a world of wild land pristine
It comes as the oldest, grandest scene

In a world of fools it came as a man with a role
In a world of children it came as a mother's
console
In a world of seeing each other as others
It came as another
Albeit with grieving,
believing a being was needed
to accept all the flowers it'd be receiving

In a world of signals, all identities linked
It comes as a consciousness, perfectly synced
It comes as our songs, our resonate words
The things that compel and those that disturb
It comes as the fears that frighten
And the things that we delight in
The things that rip our heart and mind in
As many parts as forms it hides in

Flowers do not tread lightly

Life cares not
For what is lost
Or what is got

For flowers do not tread lightly
On cemetery grounds

But simply grow where they can grow

In fact, they do so even better
When there's rot below

I met a millionaire

I met a millionaire
on the street corner
with a can of coins and a cardboard sign

I met a millionaire
who made a living
selling smiles free of charge

I met a millionaire
with a million cares
A million hopes and fears
A million bad things they did
But a million and one regretted
A million things they hope to see
And a million that never will happen
A million honest actions
and a million actual laughs
A million reasons for a million feelings felt

I met a millionaire
who had barely a care
for anything other than just
being brilliantly there

Metaphor

Tears in the rain go unnoticed
Confessions in a crowd unheard
Like words too oft spoken with no meaning
And metaphors
That fall too short

Light's Dark Secret

Not at once does darkness bring its solemn vow
But with a gradual ease, through subtle means
Hidden behind the wilted petal
Or the once more falling of the leaves

What clever trick age plays with the unknown
So cautious and slow
So not to spook, but fool
Those in disbelief of what cannot be known

Until the moment when we have
the context of years prior
We look through a filter of familiarity
And see the true force
that dark change can inspire

Though with it comes its long time child friend
Light: which holds no secret to amend
But more so, with no mercy
Presents the brutal fullness
of the moment to our eyes

Much less shy though with much more greed
For it pervades in everything we see
regardless of its nature, intent

or attempt for us to false perceive

The two well know their bounds,
for like the one pole both north and south
They remain one and the same:
Dark to save us from futility
Light to show the way

Speaking secrets with spiders

I knew an arachnid
Their name is [redacted]
(Anonymity
Must be protected)

One day we both
were feeling rejected
But with each other
We felt connected
So we made a vow, a secret pact it
was drawn into our web

Somnambulist

The house lights went out right when
the darkened garden grew out of childhood.
Mistaking alignment of all starts and ends
Fumbling, not knowing what we do and what we
should

With empty halls to roam about in
and restless states to speak aloud in

We talk of what we're hoping for
and sleepwalk through the open door

Morning Dance

Let us dance! Let us dance!
Said the ferns of the forest and the weeds of the
wood
Whose roots, though shallow, are rooted deepest
in good
And when the wind came
Since the earliest morn
Dance they would!
For to do that,
was all they ever could.

9 789360 944353